The Zela Wela Kids

Learn about Needs and Wants

By Nancy Phillips, MBA
Illustrations By, Emily Stewart

Published by DollarSmartKids Enterprises Inc. March 2011

Written by: Nancy Phillips, MBA
Illustrated by: Emily Stewart
Edited by: Ellen Beck

ISBN: 9798509533907

"Life is a succession of lessons, which must be lived to be understood."

~ Ralph Waldo Emerson

“Okay, you two, let’s make sure we stop and look both ways before we cross,” said Mom. After they all crossed the parking lot walkway, Mom asked if they would like to push their own shopping carts.

“I want to push a cart!” Emma replied happily as she ran over to the “Shopper in Training” carts.

“Jack?”

“I want a cart, too, please!” Jack exclaimed.

"What's first?" asked Jack.

"Fruit and vegetables," Mom said. "Please get us a few oranges and apples."

"What's a 'few' mean again?" asked Jack.

"Not too many," answered Mom. "Three or four would be fine."

"Then what's 'a couple'?" asked Emma.

"A couple means two, Emma," said Mom, holding up two kiwis, one in front of each eye.

They all laughed.

"What vegetables would you like to get today?" asked Mom.

"Carrots and corn," Emma suggested.

"Peas and beets for me!" said Jack as he searched for his favorites.

"Oh, we need to go back and get bananas so we can make smoothies for breakfast tomorrow. Jack, will you please go and get half a dozen bananas for us?"

Jack looked at his mom curiously.

"Half a dozen means six," explained Mom.

Jack returned with the bananas.

"Thank you, Jack. Is there any other fruit we should get before we move on?"

"Let's get some strawberries to put in our smoothies," said Emma.

"Mmm, that sounds good, Emma. They are right here, $3.00 a package. That's a pretty good price for this many berries. Do you want to choose?"

Emma reached over and picked up a big box of strawberries.

Carrots
$2.67ea
Celery
$2.34 ea
Squash
$1.10ea
Zucchini
.86¢ ea
Asparagus
$2.09 ea
Beets
.80¢ ea
Cucumber
$2.29 ea
Shopper in Training
Bananas
$1.75ea
Watermelon

"Alright, let's head this way," said Mom as they passed the freezers.

"Mom, we're out of ice cream bars again," said Emma. "Can we get a box, pleeease?"

"Okay, Emma, I did have them on the end of the list. First I want you to listen to me. Jack, please listen, too. It's hot outside and we all love cold treats. But from now on, you two will have to stick to just one bar a day. This box has enough to last for two weeks, and we won't be getting any more before then. Agreed?"

"Yes, Mom," the twins replied.

"Great!" said Mom, smiling. "Now let's go get our milk, eggs and butter!"

"Here's the butter," said Jack, holding up a brick of butter.

"Thanks, Jack, but before we put it in the basket, let's check the price. It's usually really expensive here. Look at this," she said, pointing to the price tag.

The twins saw $5.99 printed on the tag.

"Five dollars and ninety-nine cents is a lot of money for a pound of butter. I think I'll wait and see if it goes on sale later this week or I'll get it at a different store."

"Okay, let's get our dozen eggs now."

"That means twelve. Right, Mom?" Emma asked excitedly.

"Right, Emma, very good," Mom said, as she opened the egg carton.

"Why are you opening it, Mom?" asked Jack, looking at the eggs.

"To make sure there aren't any broken ones, Jack. Eggs break pretty easily."

"Yeah, like the time we were making cookies and I dropped one on the counter," Emma replied, giggling.

"Yes, just like that," Mom agreed, laughing. Winking at Emma, she said, "luckily we still had enough to make the cookies!"

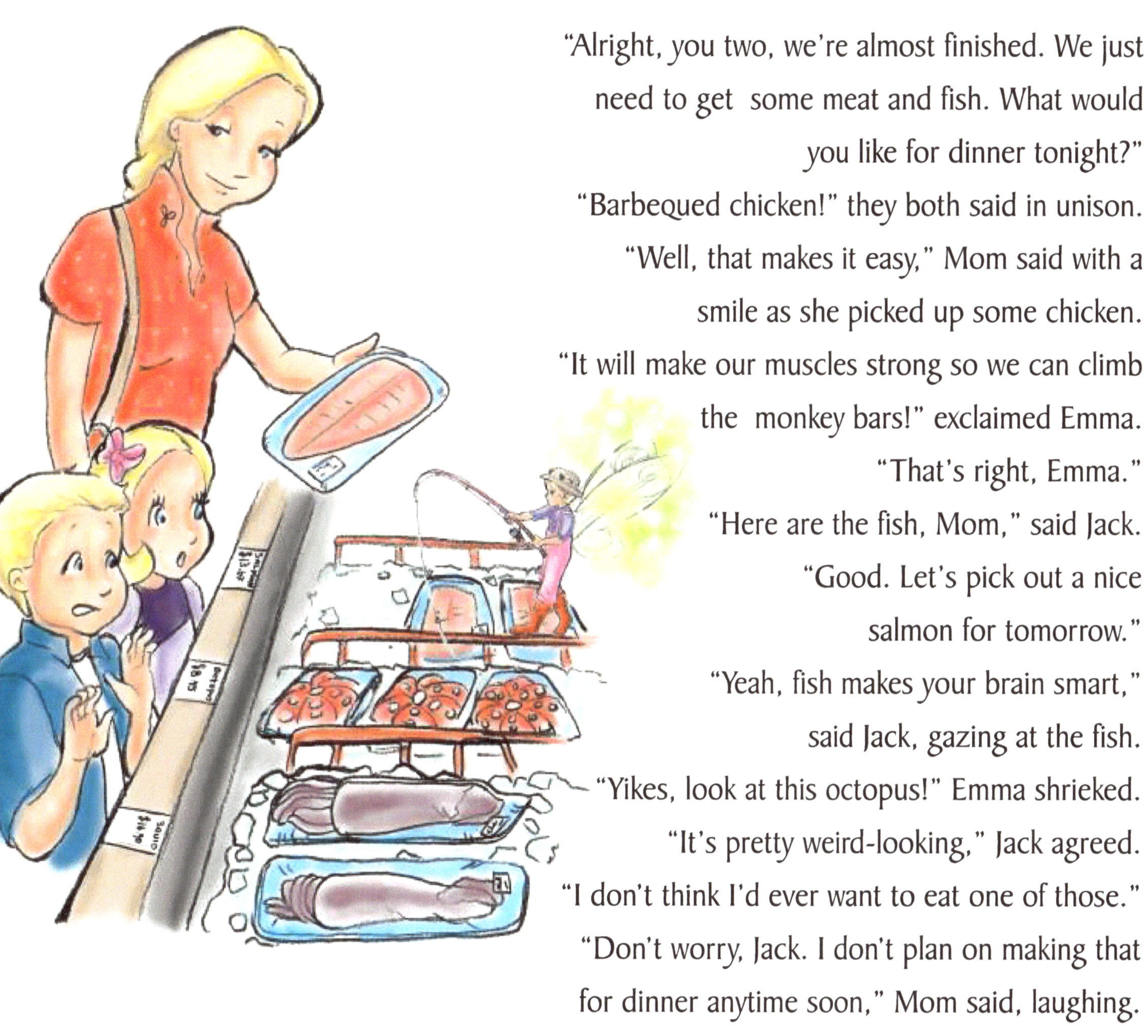

"Alright, you two, we're almost finished. We just need to get some meat and fish. What would you like for dinner tonight?"

"Barbequed chicken!" they both said in unison.

"Well, that makes it easy," Mom said with a smile as she picked up some chicken.

"It will make our muscles strong so we can climb the monkey bars!" exclaimed Emma.

"That's right, Emma."

"Here are the fish, Mom," said Jack.

"Good. Let's pick out a nice salmon for tomorrow."

"Yeah, fish makes your brain smart," said Jack, gazing at the fish.

"Yikes, look at this octopus!" Emma shrieked.

"It's pretty weird-looking," Jack agreed. "I don't think I'd ever want to eat one of those."

"Don't worry, Jack. I don't plan on making that for dinner anytime soon," Mom said, laughing.

Further down the aisle, they came to the toy section. Jack noticed a Blueback racetrack with a paint-and-wash garage.

"Mom, I really want to get this!" Jack exclaimed, running over to pick it up. "It's what I've always wanted."

"It does look fun, Jack, but it's not on our list. We're not here to buy toys today."

"Ah, Mom," Jack whined. "It's really awesome and I'd play with it a lot."

"I'm sure *you* would, Jack. You know, *your* birthday is coming up. If *you* really want this, why don't *you* put it on *your* wish list?"

"But, Mom, I want it today," Jack insisted.

"I know, sweetie, but today we are here to get the food we need to eat for the next week. We can't do without food. Stores always display things we want or desire. That's how they make money—by hoping we'll spend ours. Jack, it's impossible to buy everything *you* want," explained Mom. "You wouldn't have the time to use it or the space to store it. If *you* really want the painting garage, put it on *your* wish list along with the car set *you've* been talking about. Then *you* can decide which one *you* want more for *your* birthday. Or, *you* could save up for the garage and buy it *yourself* when *you* have enough money."

"I want the garage more than the car set," said Jack, quite certain of his decision.

"Why?" asked Mom.

"Because I already have lots of cars and I don't have a garage," answered Jack.

"That makes good sense, Jack," agreed Mom.

"How many days until my birthday?" asked Jack as he thought about his choices.

"Sixty days, which is about eight weeks."

"How long would it take me to save enough for the garage?"

"The garage is $15.99 plus tax," Mom explained. "If you save all of your spending and saving money each week, you will have $3.00 per week. Then, if you save your $3.00 for six weeks, you will end up with $18.00, which is enough to buy the garage two weeks before your birthday!"

"Awesome, Mom. That's what I'm going to do! I'll start saving tomorrow when I get my allowance."

"Good for you, Jack. I know you can do it," said Mom encouragingly.

"Now it's time to pay for everything," said Mom leading them to the check-out counter.

"Can I get one of these?" Emma asked, holding up a candy bar.

"And I want one of these," said Jack, taking a box of candies off the shelf.

"Did you both bring your spending money?" asked Mom.

"Yes, I did," said Emma, pulling out her change purse.

"Me, too," said Jack, digging into his pocket.

"You can both buy a treat then. Emma, go ahead and buy yours first."

Emma put her treat up on the conveyor belt.

"That's eighty-nine cents," said the cashier.

"Mom, can you help me?" said Emma, pulling out some quarters.

"Sure, honey. Those three quarters add up to seventy five cents. Adding one dime will make it eighty-five cents and four pennies will bring it to eighty-nine cents."

Emma put the money out for the cashier.

"Thank you," the cashier said to Emma with a smile.

"You're welcome," said Emma, taking her candy happily.

Jack put his candy on the counter.
"That's ninety-five cents," said the cashier.
"You can give her four quarters, Jack," Mom suggested. "That's one dollar, just five cents more than what the candy costs."
Jack handed the money to the cashier.
"Five cents change," the cashier said, handing Jack a nickel.

"This is all I get back?" said Jack sadly, as he picked up his candy.
"It's hard to see your money go so quickly, isn't it?" said Mom.
"I'll say!"

They unloaded the carts and then it was Mom's turn to pay.

"Fifty-eight dollars," said the cashier.

"Wow, that's a lot, Mom!" said Emma.

"Yes, groceries cost a lot, Emma," Mom replied as she counted out six ten-dollar bills.

The cashier gave her two dollars back.

"Why don't you use those ATM money cards?" asked Jack.

"I do use a debit card once in awhile, Jack, but I like to use cash most of the time—especially when I'm with you two. That way, you can see real money being spent. Money doesn't pop out of the automated teller machine just because you want more. You must earn the money and then put it in your bank account before you can take it out of the ATM. It's the same as your spending bank. If you keep taking money out and spending it, the container will eventually become empty unless you put more money back in."

"What's a bank account?" asked Jack.

"Well, first of all," explained Mom, "a bank is a business that holds *your* money for *you* so it's safe and it won't get lost. My account at the bank has my name on it and a special number so the bank knows how much money is mine. The people at the bank keep track of how much I put in the account and how much I take out. Does that make sense?"

"Yes, but if you use a card, you can get anything you want!" replied Jack.

"Unfortunately that's not the case, Jack. Whether you use cash or an ATM card, the money is taken from your bank account and you must refill the account with money you earn. If I use cash, I tend to think more about what I'm doing with my money. I only want to spend my money on things that are worthwhile, like good food or doing something special with you two. When you use a card, it's very easy to spend more money because the cash doesn't actually leave your hand and go into someone else's.

"Oh," said the kids.

After Mom made sure Jack and Emma were buckled in, she opened her purse and took out a piece of paper and a pencil.

"What are you doing, Mom?" asked Jack.

"I'm writing down how much I just spent on groceries. It's important to keep track of what you spend your money on. That way, you know where your money is going. It only takes a few seconds to write it down, and then I know exactly how much I'm spending on food, gas, gifts and all the other things I buy each month."

Daily Expenses

August	Groceries	Gas	Eating Out	Gifts	Clothes	Personal Care	Medical Exp.	Entertainment
	$58.00	$30.00	$37.00					$25.00
Total:								

After they got home, Emma began unpacking the grocery bags. Mom noticed Jack looking unhappy.

“I can’t believe my spending money was gone in two bites,” groaned Jack, pulling the candy box out of his pocket.

“You learned a tough lesson today, Jack. It can be really sad when your money disappears so quickly—especially if it goes towards something that doesn’t give you

much joy. As you just saw at the store, there are a lot of different things you could spend your money on," Mom explained gently. "Next time you want to buy something, ask yourself, 'Should I buy this now, or keep my spending money and use it for something even better in the days or weeks ahead?' Your saved money becomes your future spending money, so thinking about your decisions beforehand is very important—especially if you want to save for something special."

"I get it, Mom," said Jack, looking at his empty box. "That way, I'll feel good after I buy something with my money, instead of sad."

"Exactly, sweetheart! You want to feel good about the decisions you make. That's why you need to think before you buy. Now, let's finish putting away this food so we can play. Then, in a couple of hours, we'll eat our yummy chicken dinner and go outside to enjoy our evening!"

"What are we going to do tonight?" asked Emma, putting the fruit away.

“Well, there are a lot of fun things we could do,” replied Mom. “Let’s name some and then we can decide what we feel like doing. Emma, *you* start.”

“The beach or the park,” Emma suggested.

“Biking on the trail,” added Jack.

“Those are all good suggestions,” said Mom.

“How about we bike down the trail to the beach?” replied Emma.

“That’s a great idea, Emma. It will be a beautiful night at the beach.”

And so, after a very yummy dinner, they all went on a fabulous ride to the beach.

Fill Out Your Own WISH LIST!!

MY GISS VISION BANK

Give, Invest, Save, Spend

GISS It!

and Make Your Own GISS Cereal Box Bank

Thank You, I am grateful to have spent this time with you

Nancy Phillips

www.ingramcontent.com/pod-product-compliance
Lightning Source LLC
Chambersburg PA
CBHW042119110726
48006CB00002B/693

* 9 7 9 8 5 0 9 5 3 3 9 0 7 *